FAIRY TALES
FROM THE FAR EAST

(ADAPTED FROM THE
BIRTH STORIES OF BUDDHA)

BY

THEO. GIFT

AUTHOR OF "LIL LORIMER," "CAFE TOWN DICKY," "THE LITTLE COLONISTS,"

WITH ILLUSTRATIONS BY
O. VON GLEHN

TABLE OF CONTENTS

THE QUARRELSOME QUAILS 1

THE TORTOISE THAT COULDN'T
HOLD ITS TONGUE 11

THE WISE MERCHANT AND
THE FOOLISH 35

BIG CHERRY AND LITTLE CHERRY; OR,
THE STORY OF THE ENVIOUS OX 55

THE MONKEYS AND THE
GOBLIN POND 75

THE CRAB THAT OUTWITTED
THE CRANE 91

SELIM'S FORTUNE; OR, "SMALL
BEGINNINGS MAKE GREAT ENDS" 105

THE GOBLIN'S QUESTION 121

THE CONCEITED DEER 135

TO MY CHILD READERS.

MY DEAR CHILDREN,

If you like these stories, which I have collected and put into story-shape for you, and which come out of one of the very oldest books in the world, you must thank not me, so much as a very learned man, Professor Rhys Davids, who first translated into English the book I speak of out of the ancient language in which, thousands of years ago, it was originally written; and so made it possible for less learned people like you and me to enjoy the stories in it. That you may get as much fun out of reading them as I have done out of writing and shaping them for you, is the hearty wish of your friend,

THEO. GIFT.

THE QUARRELSOME QUAILS

THE QUARRELSOME QUAILS

ONCE upon a time there was a fowler, a poor man, with a wife and family, who earned a small living for himself and them by catching quails, which he afterwards killed and sold in the public market.

Now, the way in which he caught them was this. He used to lie down in the long grass and imitate the cry of a wounded quail; and then, when the quails came running up from all sides to see who was hurt (for quails are very sociable, affectionate birds, and live in large flocks), he would throw his net over the lot, and go off to catch some more before collecting them together in a heap, breaking their necks, and packing them into his basket; and in this way he caught very many, so many that nearly all the quail families were in mourning; and the crows did quite a good business in black feathers.

One day, therefore, the oldest father quail called all the quails together and said to them—

"My children, the fowler is thinning our numbers every day, and bringing death and destruction to us; but I have thought of a means by which we may escape him. In future, as soon as he has thrown his net over you, lie still till it has settled, and then let each one put his head through a mesh in the net and *lift it up all together*, spreading your wings at the same time, so that you may fly away with it until you come to the nearest thorn bush. Drop down gently on that, and the thorns will seize the net by its meshes, and hold it up from you, thus allowing you to slip out easily from underneath."

The quails thought this was a capital idea, and the very next time that a group of them got caught under the fowler's net they lifted it up altogether, as the father quail had told them, flew away with it, and, leaving it on a thorn bush, got off safely, as he had said, and without the loss of one of their number. As for the fowler, he had to run after them as hard as he could, and while he was trying to disentangle his net from the thorns without tearing it, the birds crept farther and farther away under shelter of the long dry grass, and were soon snugly hidden among the shrubs and bushes, so that he had to go home empty-handed.

Next day the same thing happened again; and so it did the day after next. The quails always did as they had been taught by the father quail, and so the fowler spent the whole time following them about and disentangling his nets till night fell, when he had to go home without having caught a single bird or earned any money. Now, when this had happened a good many times his wife got very angry, and, flying into a rage, she said to him—

"How am I or the children to live if you come home empty-handed every day? We have nothing for dinner, as it is, and we shall starve if this sort of thing goes on. Evidently you have left off caring what becomes of us. The fact is, I believe you have a wife and family somewhere else, and spend your money on them."

"My dear," said the fowler, "Fate has been cruel to me; but not so cruel as it might be. I have no wife but you, and no family but yours, to spend my money on. I will tell you exactly how it happens. These quails are so wonderfully united and friendly with one another that they have evidently made a plan to act all in concert and fly away with my net the moment I cast it over them. Don't get angry with me, however, this can't go on forever. Birds are quarrelsome folk. They are sure to fall out before long; and the minute they do so I shall get the better of them.

*'When friends and families come to blows,
Then is the time to fear their foes.'*
Only be patient for a little."

And, true enough, it all fell out as he said; for a few days later, as they were tumbling out of the net after leaving it on the thorn bush, one of them trod accidentally on another one's head.

"Now, then! what did you do that for, treading on my head?" cried the one who was hurt.

"What did you put your head in the way for? I didn't tread on you on purpose," retorted the other.

The Quarrelsome Quails

"No," said the injured one, "but because you were so clumsy you couldn't look where you were going."

"No more clumsy than yourself!" cried the other, "and for my part I'd rather be clumsy than an ill-tempered old baldhead."

But this made matters worse.

"*Bald!*" cried the one quail, in a rage. "And if I am bald, it is because I have rubbed all the down off my head with pushing it through those horrid meshes in order to lift the net off you."

"Off *me*!" shouted the other quail. "Well, I like that! Do listen to him, you fellows; one would think he did all the work of lifting! Why, only yesterday I lost two of the very best feathers out of my right wing in the efforts I had to make to raise the net from the ground. A fine boaster *he* is!"

And so they went on quarrelling, some of the birds taking one side and some another, till there was no one to listen when the old father quail begged them to desist and make friends; and at last, in despair of making them hear him, he said to one or two of the quieter birds about him—

The Quarrelsome Quails

"They will go on till they are all destroyed, for we quails are but feeble folks; and with so many enemies in the world, if we do not hold together, we are sure to be caught and exterminated." Wherefore, taking these more peaceable ones with him, he went off very sadly, and nestled down in a quiet corner of a sandbank under a clump of wild thyme bushes.

But next day what he feared came to pass; for the fowler came by again, and, imitating the cry of a wounded quail, soon succeeded in casting his net over those that ran together. Then one of those birds who had been quarrelling the day before cried out to the other—

"There was a great deal of talk yesterday about the very down on your head being rubbed off by the force with which you heaved up that net. Heave away now, then!"

And the other retorted—

"There was a great deal of boasting yesterday about the best feathers in your wing being dragged out by the dash with which you flew away with the net. Fly away with it now, then!"

And while they stood puffing out their plumes and mocking each other, but doing nothing, the fowler himself came back, and, lifting them and the net together, wrung all their necks and bundled them into his basket; after which he took them to the market, and, having sold them for a good price (for indeed a fat little roast quail with a piece of bacon on his stomach is a dish much esteemed by rich people), he took the money home to his wife, who this time received him with a hearty welcome. But all the quail family were in mourning again that evening; and the crows sold more black feathers than ever.

This is what comes of brothers and sisters quarrelling; for the fowler was quite right when he said—-

"When friends and families come to blows,

Then is the time to fear their foes."

THE TORTOISE THAT COULDN'T HOLD ITS TONGUE.

THE TORTOISE THAT COULDN'T HOLD ITS TONGUE

ONCE upon a time, a long while ago, there lived a King who was very fond of talking. He was quite a young man, and a very good King in most respects, brave and truthful and kind to all his people; but he had this one fault, and a fault it is in everybody, but a very bad one in a monarch.

If you don't understand how this can be, I'll tell you. When any one came to him to complain of a wrong or injustice, he was so impatient to begin talking about the case, that he couldn't even wait to listen to the end, and so very often judged it unjustly for want of having heard both sides of the matter. In the same way when somebody appealed to him for charity, he was full of pity, but interrupted the sufferer so often to tell him so, or to relate some story of similar misfortunes (which is always a silly thing to do, for if a person has a toothache it is really *no* comfort to him to be told that you had a worse one yesterday, or your grandmother a pain in her big toe last week!), that very often the beggar never got to the end of his tale after all, and sometimes the King was called away before he had time to give him anything, or sometimes gave him more help than he deserved. As to secrets, his friends had long ago left off telling him any, for he was always certain to tell them to the next person he met; and that often caused a great deal of trouble, especially in matters of state; while as to the mischief he made and the quarrels he stirred up by his habit of repeating every little thing that one person said to another, I could never tell you the half of them: and yet he had the kindest heart in the world, and hated nothing so much as for people to be on bad terms with one another.

Now, fortunately for himself, this King had a very wise old minister; so wise and so clever that he could almost hear what was said in the next country, and could count the threads in a spider's web at the top of the church steeple, and speak every language in the whole world, even those that are spoken by the birds, the animals, and the fishes.

The Tortoise That Couldn't Hold Its Tongue

Of course, to a man as clever as all that, this foolish love of talking in the young King, of whom he was very fond, was a great grief. Indeed, he spent so much of his time in trying to undo the harm occasioned by it, that, it interfered very much with his other work; and he would have given a great deal to cure the young man of it, only that that was not an easy thing to do; for to tell him of his faults might have offended him, and in those times Kings were still very great people, and thought nothing of ordering your head to be cut off if you did not pay them proper respect. We have altered all that now.

Well, one day as the old minister, whose name was Konosco, was sitting on a bench in the sun trying to think how he could best speak to the King on the subject, he heard a great deal of chattering on the other side of the wall against which he was leaning; and, looking over, he saw a tame tortoise which belonged to the King, and was allowed to run loose about the courtyard, talking to a couple of beautiful wild ducks, who seemed to have just alighted from one of their flights beside him.

"To think of our recognizing you, and when we were flying at such a height!" said one of the ducks, "it is really wonderful."

"And when we had never seen you since the day you were captured," said the other, "Ah, what a dreadful day that was! But it was your own fault. That poor tongue of yours!"

"What about my tongue?" said the tortoise, in an offended tone. "I really don't see why you should pity it."

"I pity it because it got you into such trouble," said the duck; "don't you remember how fond you were of talking and lecturing everybody with it? You were in the middle of a long sermon on the proper way to catch flies when the hunters came upon us that day. We all saw them and tried to warn you, but you would not listen or leave off, and while we had just time to escape, you were taken."

"I never heard them coming," sighed the tortoise mournfully.

The Tortoise That Couldn't Hold Its Tongue

"Your poor tongue made too much noise for you to hear anything," said the duck; "but cheer up, cousin, things might have been worse. It is something to be a King's tortoise."

"Oh, that's nothing to boast of," answered the tortoise; "for his Majesty is so occupied with running here and there and gossiping about his own affairs, that he pays very little attention to me. Sometimes I really think he forgets my existence for days together; while, on the other hand, I am the butt of every idle scamp who wants a bit of amusement, from the King's pages down to the cat; even the scullery-boy can't pass me without turning me over on my back, for the mere sinful pleasure of seeing my legs waggling in the air. I wish I could bite them. Ah dear! to be back in my own home with my wife and children, but I suppose they have died of grief long ago."

"Well—not exactly," said the duck; "though what your poor wife will say when we tell her we have seen you I don't know. You see, we all took it for granted *you* were dead long ago, and the fact is (I hope you will not be offended by hearing it) your wife is just about to be united in second nuptials to her cousin, the tortoise who lives in the sand-bank under the hill. Indeed, it is to her wedding that we are now on our way."

"My wife going to be married!" cried the tortoise, in a rage; "and you tell me not to be offended! Why, what do you take me for? And I who was the best and most faithful husband to her! Didn't I spend my time catching the fattest grubs and nibbling off the juiciest leaves for her benefit? Wasn't her shell the best polished, and her house the sunniest in the whole bank? Wasn't she always the first to go to sleep for the winter, and last to wake up for the spring? Oh, the ungrateful creature!"

"But, my dear friend, don't be so angry," said the duck soothingly, "you forget that she thinks herself a widow."

"Well, and why isn't she content to remain one?" cried the tortoise, not a bit appeased; "Isn't it better to be the widow of a handsome, well-marked,

The Tortoise That Couldn't Hold Its Tongue

lively young tortoise like myself, instead of the wife of a dull, wrinkled old curmudgeon with a cracked shell like her cousin? I'm ashamed of her."

"Truly he is old, and rather wrinkled and cracked-shelled," said the duck, "but he has one merit which one must not forget, and which your wife seems to appreciate. *You* may not have noticed it. He is dumb! It is she who will do all the lecturing now; when you were there, she said she could never get in a word edgeways."

"She might get in as many words as she liked if I were only back again," said the tortoise, much mortified. "Oh, my dear ducks, cannot you find some way to take me with you? Don't, I pray you, leave me here in this misery."

The ducks shook their heads and waggled their tails, and said they couldn't think of any way at all, for, indeed, they had a long flight before them, and were impatient to be gone; but the poor tortoise, seemed so unhappy, and so begged and prayed them not to desert him, that the good-natured birds were moved with compassion, and after putting their beaks together in consultation for a minute or two, they said they had thought of a mode of escape for him, though they were not sure that it would be a successful one.

"It is very difficult and very dangerous," said the elder duck, "and if it fails it may cost you your life; but as the success or failure depends entirely on yourself, you must decide whether you will risk it or not."

"On myself!" cried the tortoise; "how can that be? To escape from here one must be able to fly, and that is just what I can't do. If I could —"

"No, you can't fly," interrupted the duck; "so you will have to be carried; and we can't carry you on our backs, because you are so flat and slippery you would certainly roll off. Neither can we carry you in our beaks or claws, because, your shell is too hard and smooth to catch hold of; and if we were to take you by the head, it might—I don't say it would—but it *might* come off. No, there is only one way of doing

The Tortoise That Couldn't Hold Its Tongue

it, and that can only be done on one condition, which, as I said, depends on yourself. You must be able to *hold your tongue.*"

"Hold my tongue!" laughing. "Is that all? Why, that is the easiest thing possible. How do you mean?"

"I will show you," said the duck. "You see this piece of stick; now, if you take it in your mouth by the middle and hold tight, my brother will take one end and I the other, and in that way, we will lift you up and fly away with you home. It is a long journey, and I dare say you won't be a light weight; but one must do something for old acquaintance' sake, and all we want to warn you is to keep to your part of the bargain, for so sure as you open your mouth to say even the tiniest word, so surely a dead tortoise you will be that minute."

"Don't be in the least afraid," cried the tortoise, in high glee; "I am only too much obliged to you for your kind offer; and as to talking till we are safe at home, you may imagine me, if you please, as dumb as that miserable cousin of my wife's whom she, fickle creature, is thinking of marrying."

So, the tortoise took hold of the middle of the stick, and each of the ducks took an end, and after a great deal of fluttering and flapping with their wings, up they flew into the air carrying him with them, for all the world like a carpet-bag slung on a pole. His escape was not, however, to be quite as easy as he thought; for just as they were rising over the wall, a little turnspit belonging to the palace kitchen came running out into the courtyard, and, seeing what was happening, began to bark with all his might and cry out—

"Bow, wow! bow, wow! Here's the King's tortoise running away with a couple of ducks from the larder. Stop him! stop him! This mustn't be permitted. Bow, wow, wow, wow!"

The Tortoise That Couldn't Hold Its Tongue

21

The tortoise kicked out his hind leg fiercely, and longed with all his heart to tell the impertinent little dog that he was not running away with the ducks, but the ducks with him; but fortunately he remembered just in time the warning given him and only gripped the stick tighter in his teeth, while the ducks flew on un-heeding, and soon left the barking turnspit behind.

But the next place they came to was a cornfield, and there were a couple of crows, who no sooner saw them than one cried out—

"Caw! caw! caw! There's the King's tortoise flying away. He hasn't paid his washing-bill, and is leaving the country for fear of the washer-woman. Caw! caw! caw! Stop thief! stop thief!"

"Caw! caw! Are you sure?" cried the other crow, all in a flutter, for crows are great gossips, as anybody who has lived near them knows.

The Tortoise That Couldn't Hold Its Tongue

"Indeed I am. Don't you know the washing-spider who works so hard to get out all her linen to bleach before the sun rises of a morning? This morning when I was out after the early worm, the hedges were all silvery white with her work, and I said to her in passing, "You have a fine show of linen there, Mother Washing-spider; I hope you will be paid for it."

"Those who don't want to be made pay will have to fly the country to avoid me," said the washing-spider; "and now you see! there is the tortoise flying off already. Stop thief! stop thief! Caw! caw! caw!"

And they both joined in the cry, and came flying after.

The tortoise was in such a rage he nearly bit the stick in two, and did make it tremble; for though he did not dress all in black, like the crows, it was a fact that he did not wear any linen at all, his underclothing being made of yellow leather, and he had never had a washing-bill in his life; but though

The Tortoise That Couldn't Hold Its Tongue

he would have given anything to say as much to the gossiping crows, he did not dare to answer by so much as a word, and the ducks flew on steadily, and soon left the old scandalmongers behind. But when they got to the outskirts of the town it was not to be expected that they would be allowed to pass by unheeded; for it is a fact (which I dare say you may have noticed) that one does not every day see a couple of wild ducks flying home with a tortoise slung between them on a piece of stick; and great was the excitement of the townsfolk at the sight. Out ran the women from their wash-tub, and the children from their school: out ran the innkeeper from his inn, and the blacksmith from his forge; and one shouted one thing, and one shouted another, till at last an old beggar-woman who was sitting on a stone by the wayside cried out, "Eh, leave off hooting, and chuck a stone at them instead. 'Tis only two ducks carrying a miserable dead tortoise home with them for supper; and a nasty supper he will be. Chuck a stone at them, and they will let the vermin drop."

Fairy Tales from the Far East

This was too much for the tortoise. He had stood being called a thief and a debtor and a host of other things; but to be spoken of as a "miserable dead tortoise," and stigmatized as vermin, he who was the favourite of a King, and a person of dignity in his own country, was more than he could possibly endure; and, quite forgetting the ducks' warning, he shouted out—

"Miserable vermin yourself — you rude old beggar-woman! And what right have you to throw stones at me, who am not dead at all, bub a King's tortoise being carried to my home by these faithful friends of mine?"

Alas! my dear children, this fine speech was what he *wanted* to shout out. In very truth, however, no syllable of it was ever heard, for in opening his mouth to utter the first word, he let go the stick which supported him : up flew the ducks into the air released from their burden, and down came the poor tortoise—down, down, down, head over heels through the air, and fell with such a crash on the

The Tortoise That Couldn't Hold Its Tongue

stones in the middle of the market-place that he split in two, and was killed on the spot.

Now, just at that moment there happened to be passing through the market-place arm in arm the Mayor and the Priest, and very much startled they both were at the spectacle of a tortoise falling bang out of the sky on to the ground at their feet; but their wonder increased still more when they lifted it up and saw, painted on its left shoulder, a crown, which is a mark which all the King's animals in that country wear.

"It is the King's own tortoise," they said; "we must take it to the palace." And very soon the cry got buzzed about—"It is the King's tortoise; let us go with it to the palace." And off they all set in a long procession; the Mayor first carrying the dead tortoise on a velvet cushion, because it had the King's mark on it; the Priest next holding a silk umbrella over it, because it fell down from the sky, and therefore must be something miraculous; and behind them all the people in the town, rich and poor, old men and young men, matrons and maidens, boys and girls, down to even the babies in perambulators. and the babies in arms.

Great was the astonishment of the whole court, and even of the King himself, when this funny procession was seen approaching, and greater still did it grow when the cause of the excitement became known; for how a tortoise which had no wings, and was kept in a courtyard with high walls, could take to flying about in the air with a couple of ducks, as some said they had seen it doing; or how it could fall bang out of the very centre of the sky, as both the Mayor and Priest declared it had done, was a mystery which no one could divine; and the more questions that were asked, and the more explanations that were given, the greater the mystery became.

Then the King himself rose up and said, "Where is the wise Konosco, my best friend and adviser? If there is anyone who can explain this thing, it is surely he, seeing that he is the most learned man in all my kingdom, and there is nothing in it he does not know."

The Tortoise That Couldn't Hold Its Tongue

Now, the old minister, as you know, had heard all that passed between the tortoise and the ducks from the very beginning, and had been a witness of everything that followed, into the bargain, having indeed been close to the Mayor and Priest at the moment when the tortoise let go the stick and fell down into the market-place; but he had purposely kept out of the way since then; and now when he was sent for, he came with seeming reluctance, and listened to the whole story without uttering a word one way or the other. At last the King, getting impatient of his silence, asked him if he too could find no explanation of the mystery; to which the minister, bowing very low, answered humbly that the explanation was easy enough, if he dared to be so bold as to give it, but that he feared to offend his royal master by doing so.

This, of course, only made the King still more curious, and he assured the old minister that it would be impossible for him to be offended at any answer, so long as it was a true one, to a question which he himself asked; whereupon the old minister, taking the dead tortoise in his hand, and beginning at the beginning, narrated the whole history just as it happened from first to last, and wound up by saying—

"Thus your Majesty will see that the mystery is a very simple one, and so very easy of explanation that it can be reduced to five words: for, in the first place, the tortoise lost his freedom; and in the second, he lost his wife's love; and in the third, he lost his own life, for one and the same reason—HE COULDN'T HOLD HIS TONGUE!"

Now, when the courtiers heard the old minister say this, they all began to smile and wink at one another; and the King, seeing them do so (though they tried to look very grave directly afterwards), and guessing what was in their minds, grew .very red and angry, and, turning away from Konosco, asked them what ought to be done to the man who had the audacity to tell such a story as that to his monarch.

The courtiers, being anxious to please him, all hastened to say that the least punishment the old

The Tortoise That Couldn't Hold Its Tongue

minister deserved would be degradation and imprisonment for life; while some even said that death would not be too severe a penalty for such an offence; but great was their mortification when the King, who had listened to them with much contempt, answered—

"You are wrong; for if the story did not apply to me, then there would be nothing of offence or insolence in it; and if it does, then he who has courage and honesty enough to tell it at my command is a truer friend and more faithful subject than those who laugh at their King's faults behind his back and flatter him to his face."

And with that he dismissed the hypocritical courtiers from his presence, and not only rewarded the old minister, but ordered the tortoise to be embalmed and set on a golden pedestal in the centre of the palace court, so that all who saw it might learn from it a lesson of the wisdom of silence.

And so well did he learn the lesson himself, that from that day he became so much less talkative, and so much more willing to listen to others and hear what they had to say, that before he died, he had grown almost as wise as the old minister Konosco himself.

THE WISE MERCHANT AND THE FOOLISH

THE WISE MERCHANT AND THE FOOLISH

A LONG while ago, in the city of Bim, there lived two young merchants, one wise and the other foolish. Now, one day a little bird came to the foolish one, whose name was Ching-a-ring, and said to him—

"Do you know that your rival is having five hundred carts loaded with rich merchandise, which he is going to take across the desert to dispose of in the city of Chundrabund on the farther side?"

"If he, why not I too?" said Ching-a-ring. "*I will load five hundred carts with goods, and go also.*"

And this the little birds told to Ali, the wise merchant, in the same manner; for indeed, whoever else in the world is idle, the little birds are always busy. Otherwise how would all the news get about?

But when Ali heard, he said to himself—

"If this other man comes with me, we shall only hinder one another; for there is not room enough on the road for a thousand wagons, nor grass for the oxen, nor wood or water for the men; also, with so many goods the market would be overstocked and the sale spoilt for both."

So, he sent for Ching-a-ring, and explained this to him, adding—

"One of us must go first, and the other stay behind for a while. Which will you do? Think and choose."

The foolish merchant thought as hard as he could, and he said to himself—

"It must be better to go first. There will be more grass for the oxen, the roads will not have been all dug up by the wheels, nor the fruit by the wayside picked, nor the ponds muddied; and I, being first, shall sell my goods at whatever price I like. I will start at once."

But the wise merchant thought still harder, and he said to himself—

The Wise Merchant and the Foolish

"A road that has never been travelled on is sure to be almost impassable with stones and brambles. Those who go in front, therefore, will have the work of widening it and making it level enough for the wheels of the wagons.

Secondly, the oxen that go in front will have to eat off the long coarse grass, which, in the wilderness, grows on the top; while those who come after them will have the short juicy green shoots which cover the ground underneath.

Thirdly, at this time of the year the fruit is only green and the berry-bushes in flower, so no one will want to pick them; while later in the summer, both fruit and berries will be ripe and delicious for eating.

Fourthly, even where there is water in those wilds, it is often necessary to dig deep in order to get at it; so those who go first will have to dig the wells, while we need only drink from them.

Lastly, bargaining about prices with strangers is tedious work and a waste of time; therefore, if Ching-a-ring gets a big price for his merchandise, so much the better for me; for my goods are so much better than his, that when I come, I shall get a still larger one." All of which showed how wise Ali was for one so young; for, in truth, it needs a *very* wise head to hold so many thoughts as these in safety, when one is young and the bones of one's head are soft and tender. If you put too many stones into a weak basket it breaks, and if you put too many thoughts into a young head, or even thoughts that don't fit—big thoughts, wild thoughts, and thoughts with ugly shapes—it gets cracked. When one is old, and one's head is tough and hard, so hard that even the hair won't grow on the top of it any longer, then it is different: one can keep as many thoughts as one likes inside, and even change them and turn them upside down without anything happening to one. Some great men, called statesmen, do this every day.

Well, it being settled that Ali was to stay behind, Ching-a-ring started with his five hundred wagons, and soon came to the border of a sandy desert which divided the country of Bim from that of Chundrabund. Now even the most foolish know that

The Wise Merchant and the Foolish

in every desert of this sort there are places where not a drop of water can be found; so Ching-a-ring's men had loaded some of the carts with great water-pots, and filled them with water of their own accord. But what neither they nor their leader knew was that in this desert there lived a race of wicked fairies called goblins, who lived on the flesh of travellers and oxen, and used to haunt these waterless places in particular, so that they might more easily fall on those who might pass by weakened by thirst and long travelling.

So, when the King of the goblins saw the water-carts coming with the train of wagons, he was angry; but when he saw Ching-a-ring's silly face, he smiled and said—

"That fellow looks foolish enough! I will make him throw away all the water he has brought, and then, when night has come, and he and his men are hungry and tired, and parched with heat and thirst, I can easily destroy them all."

With that he waved his magic wand over a bramble-bush, and forthwith it turned into a beautiful coach drawn by twelve milk-white bulls, in which he and several of his goblin servants took their places; then he waved his wand again, and the sand on the carriage wheels turned to wet mud, and the dust on his hair and that of his servants to wreaths of water-lilies glittering with bright drops of water, and the sticks . in their hands to dripping bulrushes and branches of lotus fruit; and thus equipped, he went out to meet the merchant and his caravan.

Now, when Ching-a-ring saw this gaily decked out personage coming towards him from the desert, he bowed politely and said, "Noble sir, pray tell us if you come from Chundrabund, for we are merchants travelling thither from Bim, 'and we were told our way would lie through a desert with no water in it; but you are coming from that very desert with wet mud on your carriage wheels and water-lilies in your hair and hands! Does it rain, then, in the desert, and are there pools of water there set round with rushes and water-lilies?"

At this the goblin King began to laugh most jovially, and he exclaimed—

The Wise Merchant and the Foolish

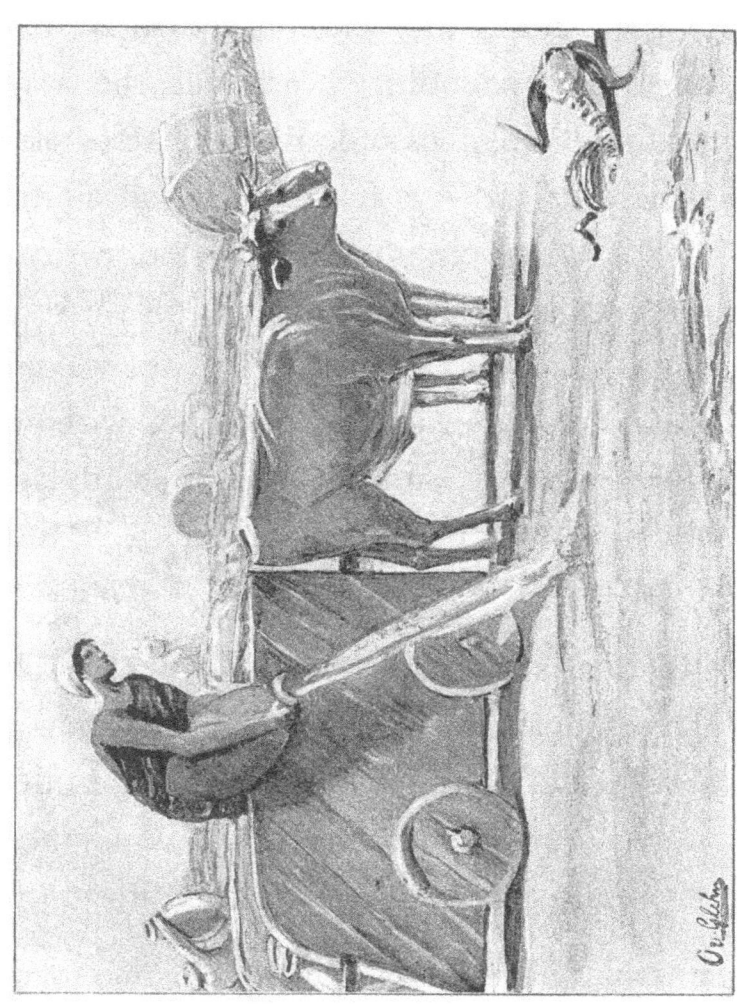

41

"*Rain*, did you say! Why, friend Merchant, just beyond that clump of rocks on the road you are travelling, and extending nearly all the way to Chundrabund, are miles and miles of green grass and forest where it is always raining; and all along the road are beautiful clear ponds covered with lotus plants and water-lilies, such as you see us wearing. If, then, those great jars, which weight your wagons so heavily and delay your journey, are filled with water, throw them all away, and travel on as swiftly as you like, for you will not need them between here and the city you go to."

"Is that so?" said poor silly Ching-a-ring, "Then I will take your advice and thank you." And with that he had all the water-jars emptied out and thrown away, even to the last cupful; and then he bade the goblin good-day, and went on his journey.

But alas! however far he went, the road lay through nothing but hot yellow sand, and red sunshine which was hotter still, and there was no water to be found, not so much as a drop; neither did any rain fall, for the sky was like a hot blue china cup

The Wise Merchant and the Foolish

turned upside down above them, without one cloud in it; and at the end of the day the men were worn out, and the poor cattle's eyes were swollen, and their knees tottering, and their mouths wide open and gasping for a drink, so that it was sad to see them. At last they were all too faint with thirst and hunger to go any farther: for, of course, where there is no water there can be no grass; and as for the men, they could not even eat the food, they had brought with them, for want of so much as a cupful of liquid to boil the rice in, or blend the flour into cakes. So, quite tired out and exhausted, they all lay down to sleep on the hot sand; and while they were asleep, the goblins and their King (who have only power to hurt men in the night time), and who had followed them all the way in the shape of a cloud of dust, fell upon them suddenly, and killed them every one, and then ate them up, oxen and men both, so that only their bones remained. But as to the carts of merchandise, as these would be no good to goblins, who could make quite as costly ones with a wave of their wand, they were left standing where they were in the desert.

Now, in the meanwhile, Ali, the wise merchant, was waiting quietly in Bim, and attending to his business; but at the end of a month and a half, he said to his men, "The fresh grass will now have had time to grow green and tall behind the oxen of Ching-a ring, and the trampled roads to harden. Also, the wild fruits and berries by the wayside are now ripe. Let us start, therefore, but take heed what I say: do not listen to what idle folks may tell you on the road, nor throw away so much as a mouthful of water or a handful of food without my permission, for who knows but we may come to want both! It is always better to have too much of a thing that is good than too little."

Which is a true saying, unless it be said of sweetmeats, because if one has too much of them, one may eat too much—and be sick. So all that day and the next they travelled by road and wilderness; and at noon on the third day they came to the border of the sandy desert; and there, lo and behold! they met the goblin King looking like a birthday prince in his carriage, surrounded by his attendants, and

The Wise Merchant and the Foolish

crowned with dripping water-lilies and lotus blossoms as he had been before; and as soon as he came near enough, he called out to them, greeting Ali most politely, and asking him whither he was bound, and what he carried in those great jars, the weight of which bore so heavily on his poor oxen.

But while he was speaking, Ali looked at him more closely, and the first thing he noticed was that this polite traveller's eyes were not blue or black or brown, but bright red, red as holly berries, or as the berries of the .pepper tree; and next, that, though the sun was shining so brightly that every little stone in the road cast a jet black shadow on the white dust, neither the strangers nor their carriage cast any shadow at all! Now, it is well known that goblins, being fairies, have no shadows, and that their eyes are red, as red pepper berries : and this indeed you may see for yourself if you meet one out walking, only it is not often that you can do so, for in these days goblins never walk out until after the dustman comes, and when the dustman comes it is time for all good boys and girls to be in bed.

Therefore when Ali saw these things, he said to himself, "This is no ordinary traveller, but a goblin;" and looking more closely, he added, "And if the water and mud on his carriage wheels were *real* mud and water, they would have been dried up before now in the hot sand and dust through which he is driving; so also would the lilies in his hair have drooped and withered in the scorching sun. These are only tricks to beguile us into some danger." On which he flew into a great rage, and, doubling his fist, ordered the goblin so fiercely to take himself off that that cruel sprite, being a great coward, as most cruel people are, made haste to get out of the way and disappear.

"But wait till night-time, and I may yet have you all the same," he muttered, as he drove away.

But meanwhile, Ali's men, not being as wise as their master, had been listening eagerly to the lying stories of the goblin attendants; and now they clustered round the young merchant, repeating all they had heard, and begging that they might be allowed to throw away the heavy jars of water which they could not want any more in such a moist and green country as they were coming to, and which only weighed down their oxen, and obliged them to move at a footpace when they might be getting to their journey's end ever so much more quickly. On this Ali smiled, and said he, very quietly—

"My men, everyone who has ever gone to or from Chundrabund has warned us of the strip of sandy, waterless desert between us and there. Has anybody till now spoken of a road lying through green forests, and beside ponds of water-lilies?"

And the men answered, "No, master."

"It would be foolish, then, to believe that the many spoke a lie and only this one the truth; and further, he says that even now it is raining hard in these forests on the other side of that clump of rocks. For how great a distance does rain cool the air?"

And they said, "For about half a league."

"We are not half a mile from those rocks. Can you feel any coolness of rain?"

And they said, "No, sir, none."

"And how far off is a rain-cloud visible?"

"About a league, master."

"We can see the blue sky for three leagues or more around us. Can any of you discover the smallest feather of a cloud in it?" And they said, "No, sir."

"In these districts there is never rain without thunder beforehand. How far off can thunder be heard?"

"For ten miles around, and farther."

"Now, have any of you heard even the most distant rumble of thunder?"

And they all said again, "No, Master."

Then said Ali, "My men, do as I bade you, and give no heed to lying strangers. These fellows were not men at all, but goblins, as you might have seen by their red eyes and their having no shadows, if you had been prudent enough to notice them as I did. It is to be hoped that my poor friend Ching-a-ring has not listened to them as you would like to do; for, if so, I very much fear he has been led away to

The Wise Merchant and the Foolish

destruction Let us journey on without any further delay, and instead of throwing away our corn and water, do not let us lose a drop."

The men did as Ali bade them, and very glad they were of it; for though they travelled all day through nothing but hot yellow sand and hot red sunshine, and no rain fell, but the sky was like a hot blue china cup turned upside down above them, they had plenty of water in their jars both for themselves and their oxen; and when nightfall came they were able to boil their rice and make flour cakes, and bathe their feet and the noses of their cattle before lying down to sleep. But when Ali saw that they were rested and refreshed, he said —

"Now, my men, we must still be prudent, for it is only at night that goblins have power to hurt men; and if they were to catch us asleep, their malice is so great there is no knowing what they might do to us; therefore, while some sleep, I and others will watch, and so we will take it in turns through the night."

And thus it came about that though in the middle of the night the goblin King and his army came upon them in the disguise of a cloud of sand, thinking to overwhelm and smother the whole caravan, and eat the flesh off their bones, when they found Ali and a party of his men standing on guard over the rest, armed and ready to defend them, the evil goblins were so frightened at their resolute aspect that they fled away with all speed, and in such confusion that one of the men said to his fellows—

"See, there is a strange thing! There is not enough wind stirring to rumple the hair of our heads; yet look at the sand blowing across the desert as though a gale were behind it."

And Ali, looking, answered—

"A cloud of sand blown with no wind to blow it is something that one cannot understand. Now, whatever we cannot understand is pretty certain to have a goblin behind it; therefore, that is not dust, but goblins." And all the men bowed their heads and said—

"Truly, Ali is the wisest of men. He is wiser than an acre of wise men. Let us call him the

The Wise Merchant and the Foolish

Wiseacre." And that is how certain persons who resemble Ali are called wiseacres even to this day.

But when the sun rose next morning they saw for themselves the danger they had escaped; for there, standing in the road close by them,, and half buried in sand, were the five hundred carts of merchandise belonging to the unfortunate Ching-a-ring, while all scattered around were the bare and whitened bones of that foolish merchant, his men and oxen.

And when Ali saw them, he shook his head many times, and sadly, over the fate of his rival; and then, as there was no one now to own the wagons, he had the most valuable hitched on to the back of his own, and so proceeded on his way to Chundrabund; whence, being safely arrived, he sent back for the other wagons; and having disposed of the whole of the merchandise for a very high price (for the people of Chundrabund were but simple folk), he found himself so wealthy that he was able to retire from business altogether, and live for the remainder of his days in peace and plenty.

BIG CHERRY AND LITTLE CHERRY; OR, THE STORY OF THE ENVIOUS OX

Big Cherry and Little Cherry, or, The Story of the Envious Ox

BIG CHERRY AND LITTLE CHERRY; OR, THE STORY OF THE ENVIOUS OX

ONCE upon a time, in the days when the great, great great-grandfathers of our great, great great-grandfathers were just having their first breeches made, there lived a farmer with one daughter, of whom he was very fond. He was a rich farmer, and his fields were full of corn and clover, and his orchards of apples and plums; and he had plenty of horses, and cattle, and sheep, and poultry, and pigs, and pigeons, and a yard dog, and a kitchen cat, and every one of them was so well fed and cared for that even the geese in the pond said, "This is the best place in the whole country to live in;" and so said the sage and onions too.

Now among the cattle were two oxen named Big Cherry, and Little Cherry, who were brothers, fine, handsome, brown and white fellows, with glossy sides and long horns, who were the admiration of everyone in the place, and who had nothing to do but eat their fill of nice sweet grass and clover, rest under the shade of the trees, or stand up to their knees in a cool, pleasant pond when the sun was out, and sleep on beds of dry, fragrant-smelling hay all the night long.

One day there was a great fuss at the farm, Men-servants and maid-servants ran to and fro, and called to each other from the front door and the back; the hens clucked, and the ducks quacked, and the little birds flew here and there twittering so fast that you couldn't even hear the news they had to tell. It was old Buttercup, the cow, who gave it out at last—

"Our young mistress is going to be married," she said; and having announced the news, she looked about her with great pride-, and added, "And what do you think? when she goes away to live with her husband, *I* am to go with her. She says she could never relish any milk as well as mine, and. so her father has promised to give me to her. Dear me! what a change it will be! New society and everything; and who can say whether better or worse—but, there! if one's mistress cannot live without one— —and the cow sighed, and gave herself such airs on the strength of her favouritism, that Little Cherry, who had a temper of his own, got quite angry, and said to his brother—

"Why should our mistress take that old thing only, and not us? Any cow can give milk; but there are no other oxen as handsome and sleek as we are. If she is taken, and we are left, I shall think it very unfair."

"How do you know you would like the place she is going to?" said Big Cherry, very sensibly; "or that you would have such good grass in summer, and such a warm shed in winter? If we knew anything about the man our young mistress is going to marry, if he were our herdsman or the cowboy, for instance, we might be sure of being well treated; but as it is, I think our home here is such a happy one, that I pity Buttercup and the poor young lady very much for having to leave it."

"As if they would do so unless it were for the better!" said Little Cherry crossly, and walked away from his brother in great contempt.

Fairy Tales from the Far East

Big Cherry and Little Cherry, or,
The Story of the Envious Ox

Next day when the cattle were being driven in from the meadows, they passed through the yard where stood the farmer and his daughter looking into the pigsty.

"Certainly, Saveloy is a fine pig," said the farmer, "and there would just be time before the wedding to fat him well."

"Oh plenty, father," said the girl; "but he must have lots of good buttermilk every morning, and apples and boiled meal. One mustn't feel ashamed of him on the great day," and she laughed and blushed a little.

"No fear of that!" said the farmer, kissing her. "He shall have the best there is to fatten him. Nothing can be too good that is to appear at my daughter's wedding."

Little Cherry had listened to this in passing, and when he got into the shed, he fairly stamped about in the straw with rage.

"*Did* you hear, brother? — Did you hear?" he called out to Big Cherry. "That ugly black Saveloy, invited to the wedding, and fed up for it on all sorts of dainties that he may look sleek and beautiful, while we are left out in the cold and not noticed! An ill-bred thing like that, who lay on his side and snored even while he was being promised apples and buttermilk, and you and I with nothing but chopped straw and grass!"

"My dear brother, don't be so silly!" said Big Cherry; "what can we want better? The grass is delicious, the clover and chopped straw of the very best quality: we have never had anything else in our lives. Why should we begin to grumble now because Saveloy has something different?"

"Saveloy has never had anything but the contents of the washtub in his life. Why should he be given anything different?" retorted Little Cherry. "And didn't I tell you it was to fatten him up for the wedding, so that they might not be ashamed of him? *I* know whom they needn't be ashamed of, if they only had the decency to invite him." And the young ox tossed his head and slapped his legs with his tail more ill-temperedly than ever. In point of fact, he

Big Cherry and Little Cherry, or,
The Story of the Envious Ox

could have wished he was slapping both the farmer and his daughter.

That night Little Cherry couldn't sleep at all for the thought that Buttercup and Saveloy were to come in for such good fortune, and he have no share in it; and when morning came, and the cattle were driven out again to the pastures, he would not go with the rest to the high end of the field where the moon-daisies and chamomile flowers grew, and where a grove of chestnut-trees made a pleasant shadow on the sunlit grass, but lingered about by himself at the bottom of the field and close to the pailing which divided it from the pigsties, till he saw Loti, the yard-boy, bring a large pailful of something which looked very good, and empty it into Saveloy's trough. This was too much for him; and when Saveloy woke up and began to gobble—which he did at once—Little Cherry could bear it no longer, but thrust his head in through a hole in the fence just above the trough, and said to the pig—

"Good morning to you, Master Saveloy. You seem to have a very good breakfast there."

"Yes, indeed, Mr. Little Cherry," said Saveloy, who was a good-humoured, humble little pig, and quite pleased at being taken notice of by the fine young ox. "Twice as good as usual it is— I don't know why. I hope you have fared as well."

"Alas! no," said the ox. "The grass is as dry as chips this summer, and the water in the pond more than half mud. If you have really more than you want, Saveloy, I shouldn't mind helping you a bit; for the sun makes me quite faint. It must be only a taste, however, mind that—only a taste, for I have no appetite at present—no appetite whatever," and with that he pushed his head farther in and began to swallow down the rich good food in the pig's trough as fast as he could.

Saveloy held back a little at first out of politeness; but after a minute or two he began to think that if this was "only a taste," it was a pretty big one, and that he'd better make haste to get in his own snout, or there would be no breakfast for him. And indeed, there was not much.

Big Cherry and Little Cherry, or,
The Story of the Envious Ox

"There, I have helped you nicely," said Little Cherry, when they had finished. "As you said, there was far too much for you; and it is shockingly bad manners to leave what is set before one. Ta ta, friend Saveloy," and he went away.

Next day the same thing happened over again. Loti, the boy, filled the pig's trough with all manner of good things, and Little Cherry waited about till he was gone; and then thrust in his head, and with a cheerful," Ha, friend Saveloy, waiting for me to breakfast with you, eh? Well, as I see they have given you a double supply" he began to eat as hard as he could.

Poor Saveloy did not feel half so pleased as at first, for the ox had such a very big mouth and tongue that he managed to put away much more food than the pig did; but then he had also a pair of such *very* long sharp horns, that Saveloy did not like to be inhospitable or say anything rude. It is never well to be rude to people—*with horns!*

Well, one fine morning the farmer and his daughter came to look at the pigs.

"Dear me!" cried the farmer. "What's the matter with the animal? He's thinner than he was before. How can that be?"

"So he is," cried the daughter; "and yet, do you know, I prepare his food myself every day, and give it with my own hands to Loti to take to him. I wonder if he spills half of it on the way. He is a very careless boy."

"Yes, he's a very good-for-nothing lad, though I give him a beating every other day, and do all I can to improve him," said the farmer. "I'm afraid I shall have to send him away;" and so they went on blaming poor Loti, which was very unjust; and all the while Little Cherry was frisking about in the field on the other side of the fence trying to attract their attention.

"What a fuss they make over that Saveloy!" thought the envious ox. "I wish they would look at *me*." And just then the farmer's daughter did.

Big Cherry and Little Cherry, or,
The Story of the Envious Ox

"Why, father," she said, "just see what mad spirits Little Cherry is in! And how big he is growing, too!"

"So he is," said the farmer—"big, and fat as well. Why, he is as round as a barrel! He must have been in my clover field."

"Indeed, I haven't," said Little Cherry; but no one understood him.

"*Indeed*, he has not," said poor Saveloy; but no one understood him either.

"One would think we had been fattening him for Christmas," said the farmer meditatively, as he looked at the ox's plump brown sides. "Upon my word, daughter, if that pig doesn't improve by your wedding-day I've half a mind to——"

"Not to have Little Cherry!" cried the daughter, kissing him, "Oh, father, that would be too good. You don't mean it!"

"Well, well, we shall see," said the farmer. "I don't like the looks of that pig;" and they went away.

As for Little Cherry, he nearly danced with joy, and couldn't resist dropping more than one hint as to what was going to happen to his brother and Buttercup.

"Don't be surprised if you learn that I am to be a guest at this wedding after all," he said. "One hears news down at Saveloy's, my friends! It is not the thing in good society to ask the grandest people first, but rather the poor folk, who require a good deal of time to make themselves presentable; but, of course, you know that!"

Big Cherry and Buttercup, however, knew nothing about the rules of good society, so they went on chewing the cud and made no answer. Cows and oxen are more fortunate than we. When they don't know what answer to give to a question, they can always chew the cud.

Next morning the farmer's daughter stood at the door to see for herself that Loti did not spill the pig's food; but poor Saveloy was none the better for that, for Little Cherry was close by, and the moment

Big Cherry and Little Cherry, or, The Story of the Envious Ox

their backs were turned, he put in his head and began to gobble up the rich mess as quickly as possible. In vain the poor pig remonstrated. Little Cherry only stared at him fiercely, and asked him what he meant, jerking about his sharp horns in such a dangerous, way that Saveloy ran off in a fright, and didn't even dare to come near him. Little Cherry knew he was no better than a robber, but he didn't care; and when people don't care how bad they are, there isn't much hope of curing them.

The farmer soon came again to look at both the pig and the ox. He shook his head at Saveloy, who indeed was fast dwindling into the mere shadow of a pig; but he patted Little Cherry on his sleek sides; and one day he brought with him his future son-in-law, and said to the young man—

"See now, isn't that a fine fellow? A baron of him would be a noble thing at our feast—and after all, I can afford it. As for that miserable pig there, it is a regular scarecrow, and I believe it has the jaundice. Come, we will make up our minds. It can stay where it is, and in honour of you and my daughter, we will have the ox instead."

Little Cherry could now triumph openly—

"Aha!" said he to his brother and Buttercup, "have you heard the news? It is not I, after all, who am to be set aside and despised. On the contrary, I am to be the most honoured guest at the wedding feast, and to be made a baron into the bargain. As for Saveloy, they call him a scarecrow, and won't have him at all."

And when he got near the poor pig, he could not help teasing him and saying jocularly—

"So, my miserable little friend, I hear you have the jaundice, and are too ill to go to the wedding. They have asked me in your place, and I couldn't refuse; but you really *should* try to pick up. You look quite wasted!"

Saveloy went into a corner of his sty and shed tears. He did not care at all about weddings; but he had had no breakfast at all that morning, and his little black sides were like a wrinkled bag with nothing

Big Cherry and Little Cherry, or,
The Story of the Envious Ox

inside it. He Felt too ill even to reproach his false friend.

But next day the farmer came into the field with two men in blue frocks. One had a very large sharp knife in his hand, and the other a piece of rope with a noose in it.

"Which is the beast you are going to kill?" said the man with the knife.

"*This one,*" said the farmer, taking hold of Little Cherry, who nearly fell down in a fit. "We were going to kill the pig, but something is the matter with him—he won't fatten; so we will cut up the ox instead, and what we don't eat of him we can sell. His joints ought to fetch a good price, for he's as fat as butter."

Fairy Tales from the Far East

Big Cherry and Little Cherry, or,
The Story of the Envious Ox

Poor Little Cherry would have liked to shriek aloud and toss them all three into the air. He did moo—he did a great deal of mooing, and Big Cherry and Buttercup mooed too for pity, and he struggled with might and main; but it was all of no use, for the three men were too much for him, and soon succeeded in slipping the noose over his head, after which they led him away to the slaughter-house and killed him.

Saveloy was fast asleep in the corner of his sty, so he never even knew what had happened, or why, after that day, Little Cherry never came back to trouble him, and he was left to eat his meals in peace, and grow round and fat again, as a little pig should be.

As for Buttercup, she went to give milk to the farmer's daughter in her new home, which was a very comfortable one, and in which she was very well treated. But Big Cherry remained at the old farm, where the grass was so good, and the clover so sweet, and the chestnut-trees threw such pleasant shadows on the warm turf; and only a year or so afterwards his late mistress brought her baby boy to see him, and put the little fellow on his back for a ride.

Big Cherry had never felt so proud in his life. He would not have envied a king.

THE MONKEYS AND THE GOBLIN POND

THE MONKEYS AND THE GOBLIN POND

FORMERLY, before the railways came, there was, somewhere in this country, a huge and densely wooded forest; and in the centre of it was a lake, crystal clear, and the depth of which no one knew; for all who passed through the forest avoided it, because of a story that went about, that deep in the water there lived an evil goblin, hideous of aspect, and with power to destroy all who came near it.

Now, in the outskirts of this great forest there lived, in the boughs of the trees, several tribes of monkeys; not quarrelsome, mischievous monkeys like those in the Zoo, who have been spoilt by too much association with ill-behaved children, but playful, innocent little fellows eighty thousand in. number, who played at ball with the hedgehogs, and at hide-and-seek with the squirrels, and were all banded together under the orders of their King—a magnificent monkey, the largest and handsomest in the whole forest, big as a young fawn, with eyes as bright as a hare, and a coat as red and curly as Reynard the fox. He was a very good King too, and took as much care of all the little monkeys as though they were his children, using all his knowledge to preserve them from falling victims to the fiercer wild beasts and other dangers which might beset them. So, one day, when they had eaten up all the fruits and nuts on the trees around them, and were talking of migrating to some fresh neighbourhood, he called them all round him, and said—

"My children, this is a good idea, and I will go with you and help you to search for a new feeding ground, only remember one thing : in every great forest there are to be found good fruits and poisonous fruits, streams of pure and streams of impure water; therefore, do not eat of any fruit, or drink from even the clearest-looking pool with which you are not already acquainted, without first asking me." To which all the little monkeys answered with one voice, "No, Master, we promise you we will not," and, waving their tails, gaily set out on their journey.

The Monkeys and the Goblin Pond

Now, after they had been wandering about nearly the whole day, and were very tired and thirsty (for though they had found plenty of food, they had not come across a drop of water in their ramblings), they arrived all of a sudden at a beautiful green glade, encircled with magnificent trees which threw a pleasant shadow on the soft grass; and in the centre of which lay a small round lake, set round with flowering rushes and tall reeds, and the water of which sparkled like diamonds in the sunshine, and looked so deliciously clear and transparent that they longed to rush and drink from it without a moment's delay. Some of them, indeed, were on the point of doing so, when the others stopped them, crying out—

"No, no! wait! This is a lake that none of us have ever seen before, and of which we know nothing; therefore, if our King is not here, we must wait till he comes up and gives us leave to drink from it." And to this all the other monkeys agreed, and sat down in a circle round the pond; though indeed it was not easy to be patient, since some of them were almost fainting with thirst, and none had had a drop to drink since sunrise that morning, when they left their homes among the big cocoanut-trees on the farthest edge of the forest.

Now, the King was not very far away, having only gone a little out of the road in his search for water; and when he came up and found the eighty thousand monkeys sitting in a circle round the lake, each one sucking the end of his tail to keep him from grumbling, he asked them why they did not go down to the water and drink; but when they told him that they had only been waiting for his permission, he was so pleased that he patted all their eighty thousand heads, and going down towards the edge of the lake to examine it, cried out—

"Children, you have been wiser than you knew. Come here, and tell me what you see."

So all the little monkeys came trooping round, and as soon as they were near enough, they saw that the soft mud all about the pond was covered with the marks of ever and ever so many feet—monkeys' feet,

The Monkeys and the Goblin Pond

and rabbits' feet, and wolves' feet, and even the pretty little pointed hoofs of the forest deer, and the claws of the wild peacocks and pheasants. Then the monkey King said—

"What do you notice about these footmarks, my children?" And the eighty thousand little monkeys looked with all their hundred and sixty thousand eyes, and said—

"They are every one of them going towards the lake, Master?"

"But," said the monkey King, "are there none coming back?" So, the little monkeys looked still harder; but no, of all the footmarks, there was not a single one coming back. Then said the monkey King—

"Do you not see what this means? If out of all the birds and animals that go down to drink from this lake not one ever comes away from it, it is evident that every one of them must have fallen or been dragged into the water and drowned. Clearly, some mischievous creature lives in the pool, and it will not be safe for us to go nearer to it."

Now, when the goblin who lived in the lake heard this, he feared lest he might be going to lose his chance of supping on those monkeys (and eighty thousand plump young monkeys would make quite a gorgeous supper for even a hungry goblin), so, flying into a great rage, and without waiting for the monkey King to say another word, up he sprang through the water, splashing and bubbling, in the shape of a huge toad with a great swollen blue stomach, pale-red hands and feet, and hideous face, white with rage, and spotted with the foam which flew out of his mouth and nostrils, as, perching himself upon a gigantic water-lily leaf, he shouted out—

"Why do you stand there, you silly monkeys, looking at my lake? What is there in the water, which is the coolest and clearest for miles round, to disgust you? Come and drink as others do, unless you wish to offend me to that degree that I shall leap on to your backs, and devour you one by one."

The Monkeys and the Goblin Pond

But this was nonsense, for water goblins have no power to hurt anyone out of the water, as even the sparrows can tell you. That is why those wise birds do all their washing in the dust of the high road. It is not such a clean way of taking a bath; but it is safer. There are some little boys who do the same thing. Perhaps the sparrows have been talking to them.

The monkey King, however, knew all this beforehand, so he was not frightened; but standing his ground, said—

"These monkeys are my children, Mr. Toad; and if they do not hasten to drink, it is not from any contempt for the water in your lake, but because they are too well bred to go down to it before me. They shall all refresh themselves from it now, however, and so will I too — on one condition."

"And what is that?" asked the water goblin.

"Oh, nothing very much; a mere joke indeed, for it is only that you will answer me truthfully the first three questions I ask you."

The goblin thought this did sound like a joke, so with his great goggle eyes fixed hungrily on one very fat little monkey, who sat in a corner sucking the end of his tail as if it were a sugar-plum, he said—

"That is an easy bargain; so do your part, and I'll do mine, I promise you. Ask away, Mr. Monkey."

Then said the monkey King—

"Is it not a fact, Mr. Toad, that you are not a real toad at all, but a goblin?"

At this the goblin scowled so frightfully that the fat little monkey in the corner nearly bit off the end of its tail with terror; but knowing that it could not alter matters to answer, he said —

"Yes, it is a fact; but a goblin may be as good a fellow as a toad. So, what is that to you?"

"Why, not much," said the monkey King, laughing; "except that it is the answer to my first question; and now, here is my second.— What has become of all those who have drunk of the lake before

The Monkeys and the Goblin Pond

us, and whose footsteps we can see in the mud going down to the water, though none returning?"

Then the goblin laughed also, and smacking his great jaws so that they made a noise like the cracking of cocoa-nut shells, he answered, "They have all been drowned, eaten, and digested, as in another minute, Mr. Monkey, you and your friends will be drowned, eaten, and digested also."

"Why, how will that be?" asked the monkey King.

"Because I have power over every one, bird, beast, or man, who stoops, but for one moment even, to the edge of this pool. Nay, if a swallow dip so much as the tip feather of its wing in passing over the surface of the water, straightway it is dragged down by that feather- tip, and I devour it. And now," said the goblin, smacking his cruel jaws once more, and looking hungrily around at the assembled monkeys, "as I have kept my word, and given you true answers to three questions, the time has come for you and your companions to be devoured also; so make haste, and come down to me."

"Not so fast, my good friend Mr. Goblin," said the monkey King, "and don't set your heart on monkey soup for your supper, for I'm very much afraid you won't make it out of."

"What do you mean, fellow?" roared the goblin. "Is not a bargain a bargain? Did you not swear that you and your tribe of monkeys would drink at my lake if I answered your questions; and do you want me to set the very jackals of the forest on you to tear you to pieces as a promise-breaker?"

"Certainly not," said the monkey King, "for we will both keep our promise and drink from your lake. Indeed, as there seems to be no other water within many miles, we should most likely die of thirst if we did not, which would be quite as bad in the long run as being devoured by you. Don't flatter yourself, however, that you are going to do that.

"But wait a bit, and you will see
How these things shall come to be."

The Monkeys and the Goblin Pond

And with that he skipped off lightly, and, keeping at a safe distance from the edge of the pond, began gathering the long rushes, ten feet tall, and as thick as a small cane, which grew in the swampy places beside it, until he had collected a huge bundle numbering eighty thousand and one; and when he had done this, he made the little monkeys sit in a circle round the lake, as they had done before, and, giving them each a reed, he told them to put one end of it to their lips, say after him this rhyme—

"Puff, puff, puff, and blow,

Air come quick, pith quick go"—

and then to blow with all their might and main. Straightway the monkeys obeyed him, and puffing out their cheeks as he did, they blew so hard and long, the pith shot straight out of the eighty thousand reeds and fell into the lake, leaving the hollow stems like empty pipes in their hands. "Now," said the monkey King, "sit where you are, dip one end of your reeds into the pool and suck."

Fairy Tales from the Far East

The Monkeys and the Goblin Pond

And as they did as he said, and felt the clear, cold water rush up through the hollow reeds into their thirsty little throats, the goblin, seeing him-self outwitted, uttered a great howl of rage, and turning a summersault in the air, plunged downwards into the lake with such violence, that he stuck head foremost in the mud at the bottom, and could not get himself free until the last of the monkey tribe, refreshed and cheerful, had gambolled off into the forest.

"Good-night, Mr. Goblin," said the monkey King; "the water of your lake is excellent, and it tastes best when sucked through a reed; but I'm afraid I can't spare you any monkey soup all the same. My children don't like being made into soup." And with that, he too capered off into the forest.

THE CRAB THAT OUTWITTED THE CRANE.

THE CRAB THAT OUTWITTED THE CRANE

ONCE upon a time, in a pleasant country, where the sun is far hotter than it ever is here, - and where lions roar in the night-time, and clumsy, long-trunked elephants stump about in the forests, there lived a crane in a big nest, which was made of sticks, and fixed in the stump of an old willow-tree.

Now cranes feed upon fish—when they can get them, that is; for a crane is a very greedy bird, and will eat anything—worms, or snakes, or insects—that comes in its way.

Well, one day, as this crane was flying along, he came to a little pond in which a number of fish were swimming about. He could see them quite plainly; for as the summer was very hot, and the pond rather shallow, the sun had dried up a good deal of the water in it, leaving the fishes all clearly in view; and the sight made him so hungry (though he had only just finished an excellent breakfast of half-a-dozen frogs and a fat eel), that he did not know what to do with himself.

Of course he could have swooped down and caught one of them in his long beak; but that would have frightened the others, who would all have gone and huddled together in the deepest part of the pond, where he could not reach them; and what he wanted, seeing so many, was to have them all, so he stood on the edge of the pond on one leg, with the other doubled up, and his head bent on one side, thinking how he should manage it, until at last a little fish—a very young one, who didn't know anything about cranes—saw him, and swimming up to the top of the water, asked- "Noble sir, is anything troubling you, that you sit there thinking so hard?"

"Why, yes," said the crane, "for I am thinking about you; and I assure you the thought troubles me very much."

"About us?" said the little fish. "Why, good sir, what can trouble your majestic head about such small creatures as we are?"

The Crab That Outwitted the Crane

"Only this," answered the crane; "that since I last came here the sun has dried up quite half the water in this little pond of yours. In a few more days it will be dried up altogether, and you will be left baking on the hot mud. It will be very terrible for you."

"Terrible, indeed! Why, what shall we do?" cried the little fish.

"Well, that's what I have been thinking," said the crane "and I think I have hit upon a plan. Close by here is another pond, a much larger and deeper one, which never dries up through the hottest summer; and as I am a very good-natured fellow, if you and your friends will come near enough for me to take you up in my beak, I don't mind carrying you there."

The little fish thought this was extremely good-natured, and swam off to tell his friends; and all the young ones said, "How kind of the crane!" and all the old ones said, "Whoever heard of a crane being kind to fish! Depend on it, what he wants is just to seize us and eat us!" And this they said so loudly that the crane heard them.

"*Eat you?*" said he. "Not I, indeed I have more food already than I can manage, without you; and to tell you the truth, though I don't wish to offend you, you are a sort of fish which doesn't agree with me, and which I wouldn't swallow at any price. However, do as you like; only, if you wish to see that I am speaking the truth, just send one of your number with me, and he will tell you so himself."

The fishes thought this was a very good idea, and they chose out one of their comrades— a thin bony fish called Goby, very unpleasant to eat, and supposed to be very cunning, because he had only one eye, which he could turn right round in his head—and commissioned him to go with the crane and report on the truth of his story. So the crane lifted Mr. Goby, who didn't like the errand at all, very gently in his beak, and flew off with him to a beautiful deep pond close by, kept cool and shaded by tall trees, and full of delicious water-flies and grubs, such as fish love to dine on; and having

The Crab That Outwitted the Crane

dropped the old fellow into it, and let him swim about for a while, and roll his big eye round as much as he liked, he took him up again, and carried him back quite safely to his friends in the little pond. Then the Goby told the other fishes that it was all perfectly true about the other pond, and what a delightful place it was; and on hearing him, the fishes all declared they would be only too glad to go there, and begged the crane's pardon very humbly for doubting him.

" Don't mention it," said the crane, in the most polite way; and taking up the first fish that came, he flew away with him to the other pond, and alighted on the stump of an old willow-tree which grew near it; but when he had done this, he did not drop the fish into the water, as he had done the last, but flung it down on a branch of the tree, and driving his sharp beak through it, killed it and ate it up in a moment, and then flew back for another. This he served in the same way, and so he did another and another, until he had made a capital meal; and even then he was not satisfied; "for" (said he to himself) "I may as well have the rest to keep in my larder against the next time I am hungry." So, he went on bringing more and more, only, instead of killing these at once, he threw the poor fishes down into his nest, the sharp sticks of which hurt them dreadfully, and where they writhed about in misery, quite unable to escape.

It happened, however, that when he went back on one of these journeys, he chanced to see a fine large crab in the little pond, and being very fond of "crab" for supper, he said—

"Come, my good crab, all the fishes are as happy as peacocks in the big pond over there. They only want you to keep them company; so hurry up, and I will take you to them."

"All right," said the crab; "but how will you get me there, I want to ask? I am too hard and round for you to take hold of, you know."

"Oh! I'll grip you, tightly with my beak," said the crane. "Never fear!"

"Your beak isn't wide enough."

The Crab That Outwitted the Crane

"Not wide enough? Nonsense! Why, just look at the size of it. You'll be as safe as if you were in your own bed."

So, the crab looked; but as he did so he saw some of the blood and scales of the poor murdered fishes sticking to the crane's feathers, and being a very wise crab, he guessed at once what had happened. Nevertheless, he was not at all afraid, but said quite pleasantly—

"Your beak may be big, good Mr. Crane, but my shell is so smooth and slippery, I shall certainly fall out of it unless you will let me catch hold of your neck in my claws. We crabs can hold on pretty tight with them, and in that way, you can carry me easily."

"Oh, any way you please," said the crane, who was in a hurry for his supper; so the crab caught hold of his neck very securely, and off they flew together, till they came to the larger pond, where the crane was just turning round as usual to the willow-tree, when the crab

The Crab That Outwitted the Crane

"Look out, noble sir! you are going the wrong way. Here is the pond, and you seem just going to pass it."

"Oh, indeed!" said the crane, with a cruel laugh." And what of that? Do you imagine that I, whom you call 'noble sir,' am nothing but a nursemaid, to carry you and a lot of miserable fishes about for your pleasure? Pray look at those of your scaly friends who are wriggling about in my nest there, and at that heap of bones below. As I have served the fishes, my dear friend, I am going to serve you."

"Are you?" said the crab quietly. "Now, do you know, I think you are not going to do any such thing. Those poor fishes have been punished for their folly in trusting you; but I didn't trust you at all. On the contrary, you have trusted me, and now you shall be punished in your turn. Try to throw me down and eat me, if you like; but take care, for before you can do so I will bite your neck in two with my sharp nippers, and kill you in a trice;" and as he spoke he suddenly gave the crane's neck such a sharp bite that the cruel bird very nearly choked, and then, frightened half out of his life, cried out—

"Indeed, my dear friend, I was only in joke. I had no thought of eating you in reality; so pray let me go, and I will pop you into the water at once."

"Wait a bit," said the crab. "There are other people with whom you have been joking who have got to be attended to first. What about those bones at the foot of the tree?"

"Oh! my dear crab, those are some bones which a strange bird flying by dropped in passing. Believe me, I had nothing to do with them."

"And what about those poor fish, still alive, who are writhing in that nest of yours among the boughs?"

"Oh! my dear crab, they are only there because, as I was going to put them in the pond, it occurred to me that it would be very rude to allow mere common fishes to enter the water before a person of your rank arid dignity, so I just set them down while I went back to attend to. your lordship."

"Oh! as to that," said the crab, "I am not at all particular about my rank and dignity; so, if what you say is true, take them up one by one now, and put them carefully into the pond before you trouble yourself about me." And as he still held the crane very tightly, the latter was obliged to obey; and lifting the poor fishes in his beak, carried them to the pond, into which they dropped straightway, and swam off rejoicing.

"And now, friend crab, let go," said the crane, his eye glittering with anger; for, indeed, he was in a furious rage at being robbed of his prey, and, though he spoke so pleasantly, what he meant in his heart was to pounce on the crab the moment it let go, and crush it to death upon a stone.

"Nay; bend down your head, that I may step on to the ground comfortably," said the crab, "You are so tall that if I let go now I might tumble into the mud and hurt myself, or dirty my shell, neither of which I should care for."

"You are a little difficult to please, friend," answered the crane; "but have it as you like." And so saying, he bent his head gracefully to the ground, when in the same moment the crab closed his sharp jaws with such a nip that the crane jumped nearly a yard into the air, and before he could even come down again, or get his features straight, the crab had disappeared into the water, and was safe out of his reach.

(Don't you know why? Ah! well, you just get a fine big crab, and put your finger between his nippers, and you'll learn!)

"Now you may go and look for the bird that dropped those fish-bones," said the crab, laughing, and scuttled away to join his companions.

SELIM'S FORTUNE; OR, "SMALL BEGINNINGS MAKE GREAT ENDS"

SELIM'S FORTUNE; OR, "SMALL BEGINNINGS MAKE GREAT ENDS"

ONCE upon a time a poor young man set out to seek his fortune. He had not a penny-piece in his pocket—nothing but an old tin can, and a bit of advice which his mother had given him in dying:—"Never pass by anything you see as too small to be noticed, or anything you hear as too trifling to be attended to, for there is no knowing in what way Heaven may send us help when we need it."

So far, however, he had neither seen nor heard anything to help him; nor had he found anyone who would give him any work to do. Even the flower-gatherers who were working in the large market gardens outside the city drove him away when he begged to be allowed to join them, so that when evening came, he was so tired, hungry, and footsore, that he was compelled to lie down by the side of the road and rest.

Now, while he lay there, there chanced to come that way a very wise man, one of the King's councillors; and as he passed by Selim saw that he carried in his palm a grain of dust, and heard him murmur as he looked from it to the distant mountains—

"Even so, 'small beginnings make great ends.'"

Very much Selim wondered what this meant, but remembering his mother's words, and thinking it might contain some help for him, he bowed low before the stranger, and humbly asked him for an explanation of what he had said, on which the wise man answered—

"My son, all the greatest things of earth have their beginnings in the smallest. Those mighty mountains could never have been but for the grains of dust which compose them, and men as poor as you have made great fortunes out of no larger capital than that dead mouse in the road there."

Selim's Fortune, or, "Small Beginnings Make Great Ends"

"Since that is so, why shouldn't I make mine?" said Selim to himself; so he picked up the dead mouse, and went on his way, until by-and-bye he came to a cottage where a woman was scolding her cat.

"Be quiet," she said, "you want some meat, I know, but I have none for you, and the cat's-meat man has not come to-day, so be still and don't tease me."

"If you have no meat for your cat, what will you give me for this fine mouse? You shall have it for a halfpenny," Selim said; and as pussy began to purr with joy and fawn upon him, the woman, who was very fond of her cat, took the mouse, and tossing him a halfpenny, sent him away rejoicing.

Selim's first thought was to buy himself some bread; but remembering how hot and dusty the flower-gatherers had looked when they drove him away, he went instead and purchased a halfpennyworth of treacle, which he mixed with cold water from the brook in his old can, and going back

Selim's Fortune, or, "Small Beginnings Make Great Ends"

to the gardens offered each of the men as they came out a sup of the cooling drink, in exchange for a single flower from the basketful they were carrying to town for the morrow's market. This the thirsty fellows gladly gave him, so that by the time his can was empty he had quite a big bunch of flowers, which he, too, carried to market in the morning, and sold for sixpence.

Selim felt quite happy now, He bought himself a pennyworth of bread, and having laid out the remainder of the money in treacle, mixed a much larger quantity of the drink, and, repairing to the gardens as before, offered it to the gardeners in exchange for a bunch of flowers, and leave to carry away any dead twigs or branches which might have been left under the trees. The men agreed, and Selim having made his gatherings into a bundle, was carrying it to town, when he passed an avenue where a man was busy sweeping up the dry sticks and leaves which the wind had blown down.

"Here, you," said the man crossly, "helping is better than staring. Sweep up these for me, and you shall have them in payment for your trouble."

"With pleasure," said Selim cheerfully; so he swept up the sticks, and knotting them together, dragged them after him in the road. He had not gone far, however, when he heard a loud shouting, and saw the King's potter standing at the gate of the royal potteries beckoning to him.

"What will you sell me those sticks for?" he said; "we have just run short of firewood in the kiln where we are baking some pots for our royal master, and five have already been spoilt in consequence. Give me those bundles of yours that I may save the rest, and name your price."

"Sixteen pence and the spoilt pots," said Selim boldly, for he thought to himself, "If he is in such a hurry for the firing, he won't mind giving a good price for it," and indeed the potter did not even wait to haggle with him, but thrust the money into his hand, bade him take the pots, and hastened off with his purchase.

Next morning Selim laid out enough money on treacle to fill the whole of the great jars with sweet drinks, and having hired a truck to carry them on, was setting off to the gardens as before, when his eye was caught by a long line of black specks dotting the mountain side, and he paused to ask a passer-by what they were.

"Why," said the man, "tomorrow is the great horse fair in the city, and those are some of the horses coming in to be sold at it. The grass and forage sellers will have good times this evening, for the poor animals arrive so tired and hungry from their journey, that the dealers are always in a hurry to buy up all the food they can for them."

On hearing this Selim turned his steps instead to some large meadows by the roadside, where two hundred haymakers were at work cutting the grass under the hot sun. When these men saw his jars of drink, they soon flocked round him, begging eagerly for some, and offering to pay when they received their wages in the evening; but Selim smiled pleasantly, and answered in each one's ear—

"Don't trouble about money. Give me only one little armful of the grass from your cutting, and leave to sell it before you sell your own this evening, and you may drink your fill. I am not avaricious."

"That you are not," said the man simply. "An armful of grass isn't much, and one can well afford to let you dispose of such a trifle before selling one's own."

So, the bargain was quickly concluded, and Selim made haste to collect his bundle o grass from each man's cutting, and deposit it in the road outside the meadow. By-and-bye up came the long string of horses; and as soon as their dealers came in sight of the first haymaker they called out to him, offering to purchase a load of his grass to feed their hungry animals.

"With all my heart," said the haymaker, "but just go on a few steps first. There is a man in the road there with a little armful of grass. Buy that and you can come back for mine."

The next haymaker gave the same answer, so the horse-dealers pushed on quickly till they came to where Selim was sitting beside his two hundred armfuls of grass, which made a hillock big enough to feed the whole troop of horses; and which he was able to sell for no less a sum than a thousand silver pennies!

Now, as he was going back to town with all this money in his pocket, who should he see but an old woman standing on a steep bank staring at something, while she clapped her hands with pleasure.

"Why, Goody," said Selim, "what is it pleases you?" And the old woman answered—

"Look for yourself, honey. Do you see those two big vessels making for the shore? Those are the merchant ships from the south which have been so long expected, and by this evening all our richest traders will have gone down to the beach to bargain for the cargoes. The captains won't get as much as they think, for the merchants beat them down; but others will make huge fortunes, and even I may get a silver penny for being the first to take the news.

"Huge fortunes!" said Selim to himself. "And why not for me as well as others, if I only knew how!" and he was still thinking over the matter when, lifting his eyes, he saw passing him a magnificent carriage drawn by four horses, and driven by a coachman and two footmen in gorgeous liveries of velvet and gold; while inside sat a fourth attendant holding on his lap a court mantle and a velvet cushion, on which reposed a costly ring.

Selim asked them where they were going, and the men told him that the carriage belonged to a wealthy nobleman who was coming up to town in a day or two, and had sent them on before to have fresh gilding put to his carriage, fresh lining to his mantle, and a new setting to his ring.

Selim's Fortune, or, "Small Beginnings Make Great Ends"

On hearing this, Selim told the men that if they would only drive him down to the shore first, and let him have the loan of the mantle and ring for a couple of hours, he would pay them a thousand silver pennies. At first the attendants hesitated, but the thought of the money tempted them; and when Selim pointed out that he could not possibly rob them, seeing that they were four to one, they consented, and did as he requested.

Directly they arrived at the beach, Selim sent off two of the attendants to summon the ships' captains to speak with him, and announced himself to them as a wealthy merchant who was prepared to buy up the whole of their cargoes then and there for eight thousand gold piastres. The captains declined, assuring him that the cargoes were worth at least fifteen; on which Selim said shrewdly—

"That may be, but you know well you would not get a third of that, if you had to bargain with a number of us, and perhaps some of your goods would not be sold at all; so you will do well to accept my offer while it is still open; and as a guarantee of the purchase money, see here my signet ring, which, before I return to town, I can deposit with you."

When the captains saw the ring, which was a ruby as big as a pigeon's egg, and the grand coach and attendants, they thought they were not likely to find any customers with more money to spare than this lordly personage in the court mantle, so they accepted his terms without more ado; and thus when, an hour later, the real city merchants arrived all agog to buy up the rich cargoes, they found them already sold to a person none of them knew; and he drove so hard a bargain with them (for it would have ruined their credit to go back empty-handed) that what he had bought for eight thousand gold piastres he managed to sell to them for thirty thousand, not a penny less.

Behold poor Selim, then, now almost the richest man in the whole province; and, being a grateful fellow, the first use he made of his wealth was to seek out the wise old councillor, and offer him a present of a thousand piastres in return for the axiom

Selim's Fortune, or, "Small Beginnings Make Great Ends"

which had been the making of his fortune. But when the aged man heard his story, and how wonderfully he had profited by his mother's advice, and those few words spoken by the roadside, he would not take the money, but bestowed on the young man his own daughter in marriage, and, taking him to the King, he entreated the latter to give him the post of keeper of the royal treasury, saying that one who knew so well how to manage his own affairs was worthy to manage those of a kingdom. So, Selim was made treasurer, and lived in honour and wealth all the rest of his life.

THE GOBLIN'S QUESTION

THE GOBLIN'S QUESTION

ONCE, very far away, there lived an old King, who had been twice married. His first wife had two sons, the elder of whom was so wise and good, even when he was quite a little baby fellow, that the people called him Prince Celestial; but when the second was born, the poor mother died, and so the baby was called Moon Prince, because the little child came like a tiny light to shine in his father's night of sorrow.

By-and-bye, however, the King married again, and then another son was born—such a beautiful, laughing, golden-haired boy, that his mother called him Prince Sunshine, and the King, in his delight, told her she might ask anything, in the world as a present for him, and he would give it her.

Now, the new Queen was a very crafty, covetous woman, so she was afraid to ask for anything just then, lest by-and-bye she should think of something still bigger and better. And accordingly, she thanked the King, and said she would come for her gift some other time— there was no hurry about it.

Meanwhile, however, the two other boys were growing bigger every day, after a way boys have, and every day the people grew fonder of Prince Celestial for his wisdom and goodness, and of the Moon Prince for his weakness and gentleness, till the Queen, who had never liked them, grew so jealous for her own child, that one day she put on her most glittering golden crown, and her softest velvety robes, and went and knocked at the King's door.

"Come in," said the King. So, the Queen came in, and sitting down beside him, said in her pleasantest voice, "I have come to ask for the present which you promised me for my darling Sunshine on the day he was born."

Now, the King had forgotten all about the present; however, when he was reminded, he said—

"Well, what is it? Have you decided what you will have?" And the Queen answered—

The Goblin's Question

"Yes; give me this kingdom that you reign over, for him to rule and be King in, after you are gone."

But at this the King frowned, and said angrily—

"You have asked what is not mine to give. My other two sons have the first right to it. Go away, my Queen; you should not have wished for such a thing."

The Queen went away very much offended; but she was one of those people who never give up anything they have once made up their minds to have; and after a time she made the same request to the King, renewing it again and again; and every time he refused she went away looking so evil, that he got to fear that she might do some harm to the boys out of spite; and being old and weak, and not wanting to quarrel with her, he called his eldest son to him one day in private, and said to him—

"My son, when Prince Sunshine was born, I promised his mother a gift, and now she asks for the kingdom for him after I am gone. This I will not give her; but she is clever and cruel, and I fear she may plot some mischief against you in revenge. Take your brother, therefore, now, and fly with him to the forests for a while. When I am dead you can come back and reign in my place, as is your right, and the people will guard you on your throne, for they love you already."

Celestial kissed his father, and obeyed without a murmur; and that very night he and Moon Prince left the castle. It happened, however, that as they were making ready to depart, little Sunshine woke up, and seeing them putting on their caps and boots, asked where they were going. Celestial told him they were being sent away; and Sunshine, who was very fond of his brothers, declared that if that was so, he would go too. So, the three set off together.

They travelled away all that night, Celestial carrying little Sunshine whenever he was tired; and just as morning dawned, they reached the palm forests, at the foot of the Mountains of the East, and, dusty and foot-sore, sat down to rest.

The Goblin's Question

Celestial was the most tired of the three, because Sunshine was very heavy to carry, and he had given a hand to help Moon Prince besides; so, after they had sat still for a little, he said—

"Sunshine, dear, yonder I see a pond shining through the trees. Go and have a nice bath and refresh yourself; and when you have done so, bring a drink of water in a lotus leaf to brother and me."

Now, it so happened that in the pond he spoke of there lived a goblin, who had power to drag down and devour all those who touched the water, unless they could answer rightly some particular question he put to them; and the question this goblin chose to ask was—

"What is the greatest and grandest power in all this world?"

Not a very easy question to answer, I daresay you think; and so did poor little Prince Sunshine, who had run off to the pond directly his brother told him to do so; for no sooner did he reach the water, and dip in his hand for a drink, than he was horrified to find himself face to face with a hideous brown goblin, with ears like a bat, and long claws at the end of his fingers, who shot out of the water, and clutching him in his long wiry arms, threatened never to let him go unless answered him the question which he then put to him.

And Prince Sunshine, though he was so pretty, was only a silly little boy, and had been too much spoilt by his mother to learn; so, after he had puzzled about it a little, he said—

"The thunder that comes on the back of the storm, and sends the lightning before it to split open the biggest trees, and makes everyone tremble with fear, is the most powerful thing I know, and so must be greater and grander than anything else;" and as soon as he had said it, the goblin clutched him tighter, and dragged him down into his cave under the water.

Meanwhile, Celestial and his brother were waiting for the cool drink Sunshine was to bring back; and when he did not return, they thought he

The Goblin's Question

must be playing in the water, and Celestial sent Moon Prince to call him. The Moon Prince ran off very willingly; but when he got to the pond he could see no sign of his brother, and no sooner did he scramble down to the brink, and stoop his face to the surface of the water, so as to see if by some sad accident Sunshine lay drowned beneath, than up rose the ugly goblin, and seizing hold of him, vowed to drag him down to his cave below, unless he could answer the same question.

Moon Prince knew rather more than his brother; but even he did not know very much, because his mother having died when he was a baby, he had no one to teach him, which shows what a terrible thing it is for a little boy to lose his good mother. So, though he thought very hard, all he could say was—

"The blue sky overhead is bigger than anything else, for it goes farther than any bird can fly, and it is powerful enough to hold the earth under its feet, and the sun and the moon in its arms, so it must be greater and grander than all else beside." But, alas!

this was wrong too; and no sooner had he said it than the goblin gripped him tight, and dragged him down through the water to his cave.

Celestial sat on the bank waiting; but when some time had passed, and his brothers did not reappear, he became afraid lest something should have happened to them, and went off in search of them.

Near the pond, sure enough, he soon found the marks of their feet; but close to these there was also the print of a large hand with claws in the soft mud, and Celestial felt sure that his brothers' little fingers had never made that, and guessed that some wicked sprite or goblin had carried them off; therefore, before going farther, he knelt down, and closing his eyes, prayed for help and wisdom to rescue them. When, however, the goblin saw this, and that Celestial did not touch the water, he was afraid that the Prince might escape him, and taking advantage of the moment that his eyes were closed, he slipped out of the pond, and disguising himself as an old peasant woman, he came up behind the youth, and said to him—

"Good morrow, my lord Prince. You must have travelled far this morning, for you look sadly tired and dusty. Why do you not bathe yourself in this beautiful pond? The water is cooler than anywhere else, and the fruits of the lotus plants that grow in it are excellent to relieve one's hunger."

Celestial thanked the pretended old woman politely, but as he did so, he happened to espy a long brown hand with sharp claws showing beyond her cloak; and guessing at once that the creature was the same as had carried off his brothers, and not a woman at all, he sprang forward, and exclaimed—

"Miserable imp! it is not fruit or water that I want, but my dear brothers; and it is you who have got possession of them, and would like to do the same by me. Do not attempt to deny it, but give them back to me at once, or I shall find out a way to punish you."

At this the goblin trembled with rage, and throwing off the disguise, which was no longer any use to him, said—

"Since you are so wise as to know that I have got your brothers, go and fetch them for yourself.

But know this much more: unless you are wiser still, and can first answer the question I ask you, you will never get them."

"Let me hear the question, then," said Celestial; and the goblin asked him, as he had done the others—

"What is the greatest and grandest power in all the world?"

Then Celestial lifted up his eyes to heaven, and was silent for a moment; and after that he smiled, and turning to the goblin, said—

"The pure of heart, who scorn to sin,
The kind and true in word and deed,
These be the powers in this world
Most truly great and grand indeed."

When the water goblin heard this, he knew that his evil power was gone, for Celestial had told him the right answer; and bowing down before the Prince, he acknowledged him for his master, and offered to give him back both his brothers, if he might only live with him and wait on him.

Celestial agreed to this, on condition that the goblin would never try to harm anyone again; and the latter, diving down into the pond, straightway brought up Moon Prince and Sunshine, looking very much bewildered, because the water was in their eyes, and they could not see what was being done to them, but otherwise none the worse for their bath.

After that the three Princes lived in the forest for some time, the goblin waiting on them, and bringing them fresh lotus fruits and moor hens' eggs from their nests among the rushes, till one day the news reached them that the jealous Queen was dead. Indeed, she had died of grief for the loss of her darling boy and when Prince Celestial heard this, he knew that it was no longer necessary *for him* to hide in the forest, but took his brothers, and made haste to return with them to the city.

The King, their father, was still alive, and overjoyed to see them; but, as he was very old and feeble, he did not live very long afterwards. And after his death Celestial became King, and reigned with much honour and dignity, being beloved by his brothers and all the people.

And the goblin? Why, the goblin had grown so fond of the brothers, that he could not bear to be parted from them; and when they returned to Court, he went too, and took up his abode in the royal fountains forever afterwards.

THE CONCEITED DEER

THE CONCEITED DEER

ONCE upon a time, there was an old deer who lived in the great forest that lies to the north of India. He was so old, and had so many branches on his horns, that all the other deer in the forest had made him their King; and he had two sons, the one a very beautiful young deer with the widest branching horns, the softest, most velvety eyes, and the slenderest legs ever seen, who was called Beauty; the other, a clumsy- looking beast, with short horns and thick legs, called Brownie.

Now, one day when the spring was coming, and the young corn was getting green, and the flowers beginning to open in the meadows, the old deer called all the whole herd round him, and said to them—

"My children, you know that for a great many years I have taken care of you and ruled over you as well as it was possible to do. I have always led you where there was the sweetest grass and the purest water. I have found out for you the best plantations of infant trees, so that you might feast on the young green shoots; and I have never allowed you to wander into thickets or marshes where tigers and crocodiles hide in the hope of pouncing on us; and have even taken care to find out beforehand where the hunters set their traps, so that you should not fall into them unawares. Now, however, I am getting too old for this. My eyes are so dim, and my bones so feeble, that I am only able to take care of myself; and therefore, I have determined to place you under the command of my two sons, who are quite old enough to look after you and provide for your safety. This is the time of greatest danger. The spring is here; the corn is green; fruit and vegetables are ripening; and men, knowing how fond we are of these nice things, go out everywhere and dig pitfalls, or set traps on the outskirts of the forests, in which many of our young deer have already been caught. You, therefore, Beauty, my son, take five hundred of the herd, and you, Brownie, take the other five hundred, and lead them up into the mountains, where you will be in safety during the summertime; and when the rains begin, and the crops are cut, you can return to me.

The Conceited Deer

Remember three things, however. Do not delay to start, for every day lost is a danger added. Do not go near any house or village on your route; and do not travel by day, or even by dawn or evening, for then the huntsmen are out, and if they chance^ to espy you, you may be slain.

The two young deer promised to obey, Beauty with a great deal of pride and pleasure in his new dignity, and Brownie in his usual dull, quiet way; but nevertheless, when Beauty had selected his followers, who were all delighted to serve under their handsome young lord, it was the younger brother who was the first to put himself at the head of the party left to him, and call on them .to prepare for the march; and when some of them rebelled and said they would rather follow the noble Beauty, and others asked what they had done to be put under the rule of his ugly and dull-witted brother, Brownie only answered," The King, my father, ordered it," and bade them get ready without delay.

Fairy Tales from the Far East

The Conceited Deer

At this there was still more murmuring, many of the herd urging that *at lea*st they might wait till Beauty and his followers started. They would be sure to do so soon, and it would be most improper for those under a younger and inferior chief to take the lead; but Brownie said again, "The King, my father, ordered it," and, without waiting to hear any more, turned his head towards the open country, and led his followers right out of the forest.

They travelled all that night, so that when morning dawned they had gone quite a long distance, and were tired enough to be glad to rest when Brownie called a halt; but when nighttime came, and he wished them to set out again, some of the deer began to complain afresh, and begged him to let them stay where they were a little longer, so as to allow Beauty and the rest of the herd to come up with them; while others grumbled dreadfully at having to travel all through the dark, gloomy nights, when everything looked dismal and cold, instead of in the fresh, bright, morning.

"Besides, men do not go out to hunt so early," they said. "It is only being foolish and cowardly to travel at night for fear of them." But Brownie merely answered—-

"The King, my father, ordered it. What you say may be very good and wise, but my father is wiser than any of us; and as I am only a poor dull fellow myself, I think my best wisdom is to do as he has told us." So, saying he led them on; and as deer always follow their leader, whether they like him or not, the herd trotted after. So, travelling by night and sleeping by day, they all reached the mountains at last in safety, and without losing one of their number.

Beauty, in the meanwhile, and the rest of the herd, had not started nearly so soon.

"One day makes no difference," said he; "and as my father has made me King in his place, it is proper that my courtiers should pay me homage before we set out." So the vain young deer reclined on a grassy bank, while all the rest of the troop crowded round to pay him compliments, and one

The Conceited Deer

brought him a bunch of sweet grass, and another a tuft of young leaves, and two or three of them (seeing how very much he liked these attentions) started off to the neighbouring fields to get him a mouthful of green corn; but, unfortunately, while they were thus delaying, the farmers had seen marks of deer's feet hard by their corn-fields, and had dug deep pits, with a sharp stake in each, along the way the footmarks went; so that when the deer came out of the forest in the twilight to steal the corn, they fell into these pits, and the stakes running into them, they could not get out again, but were killed on the spot.

When this sad news reached Beauty, he was dreadfully shocked, and, being afraid lest his father should reproach him, he determined to start at once. So, he called his followers together, and they set out without any more delay. As the night was far gone, however, they had not travelled far when morning broke, and one of the deer said to Beauty—

The Conceited Deer

"My lord, would it not be very foolish to stop now, when we have only gone such a little distance? I know the King your father forbade us to travel except by night; but surely he forgot that when it is dark one cannot go half as quickly as in the light; and, besides, none of the other animals can see your lordship's beauty, or the fine appearance we make as we pass."

Now, Beauty, who was very conceited, was made still more so by this speech. "Certainly," he thought to himself, "they must think me wiser than my father, or they would not ask me to judge for myself, and therefore I had much better do so, instead of just following out the old King's orders. And, besides, since I am so handsome, and have such magnificent horns and lovely legs, it is decidedly selfish not to let other animals enjoy the sight of me;" on which he said in his grandest manner, "We will go on a little longer," and trotted forward with the rest of the herd behind him.

Unfortunately, just as they were crossing the brow of a hill, they were espied by three huntsmen who had lost their way in the hunt the evening before, and were then returning home with their dogs. In a moment they had put their horns to their lips and their spurs into their horses.

The dogs sprang forward, the huntsmen galloped after; and before the deer knew they were pursued, they were being chased over hill and dale, and forced to swim rivers and scramble through bog and briar. Some were drowned in the river, and some got pulled down by the dogs; and some got stuck in a bog and had their throats cut by the hunters' knives; and some got separated from the rest of the herd, and never found them again; so that when at last Beauty succeeded in getting away and finding shelter in the depths of a friendly forest, barely half of his followers were left to him, and many of these were more dead than alive.

Yet even this severe lesson was not enough for the foolish young deer. For a day or two, indeed, he and his friends were very careful to keep themselves well-hidden during the day, and only creep through the country at night; but as no fresh sign of danger

The Conceited Deer

appeared, Beauty's courage and conceit soon began to rise again, and before long brought him into fresh difficulties. For one fine night, as he and his followers were wending their way through a little wood, they came out close to a large farm, with a garden full of young lettuces and vines. Some of the deer were frightened, and wanted to go back, reminding their leader of what the King had said; but Beauty would not listen to them.

"How silly you are!" he said. "Why, there is not a soul to see us. The farmer and his men are all asleep, and I am fairly thirsting for a fresh lettuce, or a meal of those young vines. Surely a fine young deer like myself must know better than one who is too old even to travel. Besides, we are within an hour's journey of the mountains; so, let those who are not cowards follow me;" and down he went into the garden, with a number of his fellow-deer at his heels. In another minute they were all feeding so greedily that they had even forgotten to keep a look-out; when suddenly there was a loud shout, and a number of men and boys rushed in on them from all sides, armed with sticks, ropes, and guns. The farmer had seen them from an upper window, and calling his servants, had bidden them surround the garden quietly, so as to entrap the thieves before startling them.

In vain the poor deer tried to escape. A few, indeed, did break through the hedge and get away; but some were shot, and some were stoned, and some lassoed; and poor, foolish Beauty himself had one of his slender legs broken by a blow from the butt-end of a gun, and an eye injured with a stick. He was so much hurt, indeed, that his captors thought it better to kill him; so they did so, and next day his pretty spotted hide was taken off and made into a hearthrug for the farmer's wife.

When autumn came, and the crops were cut, and gathered, there was no vain young Beauty to lead his herd back to the big forest. Brownie, indeed came down from the mountain, bringing all his troop safe and sound behind him; but only a miserable few of Beauty's followers found their way back to their old home, and when the old King saw them, he said—

The Conceited Deer

"It is better for youth to be humble and obedient than clever and conceited like poor Beauty. My son Brownie has taken care of five hundred; therefore, now he can take care of the whole herd." And when, shortly afterwards, the aged deer died, Brownie was made King, and reigned in the forest in his stead for many years.

THE END.

www.ingramcontent.com/pod-product-compliance
Lightning Source LLC
Chambersburg PA
CBHW081747100526
44592CB00015B/2324